Santa Got Stuck in the Chimney

20 Funny Poems Full of Christmas Cheer

Written by
Kenn Nesbitt & Linda Knaus

Illustrated by
Mike & Carl Gordon

Meadowbrook Press
Distributed by Simon & Schuster
New York

Contents

Mall Crawl 1

December Substitute 2

The Third-Grade Christmas Play 4

Snow Day 6

Winter Wonderland 8

Wet Christmas 9

Dear Santa, Here's My Christmas List 10

Dear Santa Claus 12

Melinda Made a Snowman 14

The Stockings Were Hung 15

Santa's Beard 16

Rudolph 19

Santa Got Stuck in the Chimney 20

Our Christmas Tree's Embarrassed 22

Christmas Sale 23

Christmas Dinner 24

Potluck Christmas 25

The Day after Christmas 26

December 26 27

Resolutions 28

Mall Crawl

We went to the mall the day after Thanksgiving
to purchase the Christmas gifts we would be giving.
My mother, my father, my sister, and I,
we all had our lists of the presents we'd buy.

We got up at dawn and went straight to the mall,
but came home without any presents at all.
For though we were there from the morning till dark,
we spent the day looking for someplace to park.

December Substitute

Our substitute is strange because
he looks a lot like Santa Claus.
In fact, the moment he walked in
we thought that he was Santa's twin.

We wouldn't think it quite so weird,
if it were just his snowy beard.
But also he has big black boots
and wears these fuzzy bright red suits.

He's got a rather rounded gut
that's like a bowl of you-know-what.
And when he laughs, it's deep and low
and sounds a lot like "Ho-ho-ho!"

He asks us all if we've been good
and sleeping when we know we should.
He talks of reindeer, sleighs, and elves
and tells us to behave ourselves.

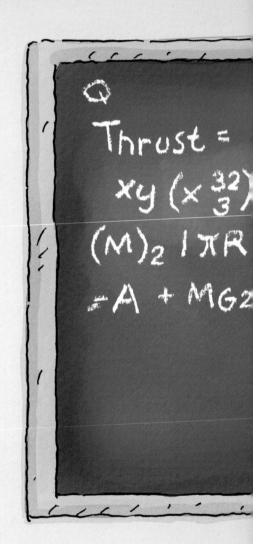

And when it's time for us to go
he dashes out into the snow.
But yesterday we figured out
just what our sub is all about.

We know just why he leaves so quick,
and why he's dressed like Old Saint Nick
in hat and coat and boots and all:
He's working evenings at the mall.

The Third-Grade Christmas Play

My mother drops me off at school.
I shout, "Hooray! Hooray!
Today's the day I'm starring in
the third-grade Christmas play!"

I'm all decked out like Santa Claus
and looking kind of weird.
I'm dressed in red from head to toe
with mustache, wig, and beard.

There's rouge upon my cheeks and ears
and also on my nose.
I'm patting on my belly
while I practice ho-ho-ho's.

I'm wearing big black rubber boots,
a shiny leather belt,
and soft white winter mittens
that my mom cut out of felt.

I'm ever so embarrassed,
asking friends for clothes to borrow.
I just found out the Christmas play
is not until tomorrow.

Snow Day

"Snow day!"
Fred said.
"All play.
Let's sled!

"No school!
Just snow.
Way cool.
Let's go!"

Fred ran
in shed.
Had plan.
Got sled.

"Go slow,"
Mom said.
"I know,"
said Fred.

Up hill
went Fred.
Down hill
Fred sped.

Sled streaked
on past.
Mom shrieked,
"Too fast!"

Snow blew.
"Can't see!"
Fred flew.
Hit tree.

Sled bent.
Fred's head
got dent.
Poor Fred.

He cried.
Now plays
inside
snow days.

Winter Wonderland

Our Christmas décor
is the best on the block,
with big plastic candy canes
lining the walk.

Huge holly sprigs circle
a wreath flocked with snow,
which hangs on the door with
a red velvet bow.

A flashing *Noel* is
spelled out near the hedge.
A snowman's lit up on
the balcony's ledge.

The roof's got eight reindeer
all lined up in twos
and pulling a sleigh trimmed
in twinkling hues.

The eaves are all frosted
with icicle lights.
Our house is the greatest
of Christmastime sights.

My dad says, "Enjoy it.
It's coming down soon."
"I hope so," I told him.
"It's practically June!"

Wet Christmas

"Is it snowing outside?"
I expectantly cried.
"What's that sound? Do you know?
Is that Santa I hear?"

"There is nothing outside,"
Mother calmly replied.
"It's not Santa or snow.
No, it's only rain, dear."

Dear Santa, Here's My Christmas List

Dear Santa, here's my Christmas list.
I hope you'll bring it all.
I've only asked for gifts my parents
can't find at the mall.

I'd like to have a UFO
with aliens inside
and maybe a *Tyrannosaurus rex*
that I could ride.

A ninety-nine-foot robot
is a present I could use.
I'll also need a time machine
and rocket-powered shoes.

Please bring a gentle genie
who will grant my every wish,
and don't forget a wizard's wand,
and, yes, a talking fish.

Of course, I'll need a unicorn,
and won't you please provide
a dragon and a castle
in the English countryside?

Of course, the weight of all these things
might cause your sleigh to crash.
If that's the case, dear Santa,
please feel free to just bring cash.

Dear Santa Claus

I don't believe in Santa Claus
like many other folks.
I think you're just a fairy tale.
I think you're just a hoax.

I don't believe you're keeping track
of who's been bad or good.
I don't believe you know if I've
been sleeping when I should.

I don't believe that reindeer fly.
I don't believe in elves.
I think the toys beneath our tree
were bought from toy-store shelves.

I once believed when I was six;
at seven I know better.
But if I'm wrong and you exist,
please disregard this letter.

Melinda Made a Snowman

Melinda made a snowman,
which she gave a carrot nose.
She placed some rubber boots
on what she figured were his toes.

Melinda gave him charcoal eyes,
and after one last pat,
upon her snowman's frozen head
she placed her father's hat.

She thought him nearly finished,
and then as a final note,
she took her father's favorite tie
and draped it 'round his throat.

Melinda was so proud of him,
she rushed upstairs with glee.
She hollered to her mom and dad
to "Hurry, come and see!"

But by the time they came downstairs
Melinda cried and cried.
"Melinda," Mom and Dad said,
"snowmen must be made outside."

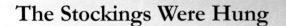

The Stockings Were Hung

The stockings were hung
by the chimney with care—
I had worn them all week,
and they needed the air.

My underwear, too,
were in need of a spritz,
but the washer and dryer
were both on the fritz.

On washer! On dryer!
The switches are busted,
corroded, eroded,
and totally rusted.

I tried hard to fix them.
I tried and I failed.
So then on the mantel
those stockings were nailed.

They hung there all year,
and then lo and behold,
Santa filled them with riches
much better than gold.

For jolly St. Nicholas
stuffed every pair
with cash for the washer
and dryer repair.

Santa's Beard

He wasn't too good with a razor,
and so every time he would try
Kriss Kringle would cut himself shaving
so badly it caused him to cry.

The townspeople laughed when they
    saw him
with cut marks all over his face.
He felt so embarrassed and foolish,
he'd lower his head in disgrace.

So one day he threw out his razor,
and all of the townspeople cheered!
No longer would Santa be shaving.
Instead he was growing a beard!

But though he has given up shaving
and grown out a beard white and thick,
most folks still remember those cut marks,
and that's why they call him "St. Nick."

16

Rudolph

The reindeer envy Rudolph for
the things he gets to do.
He's always front and center with
the least obstructed view.
It's nice up there in Rudolph's spot.
The air is crisp and clear.
The other reindeer miss so much
on Christmas Eve each year.
The reindeer envy Rudolph for
the place he's been assigned.
For all they have in front of them
is someone's big behind.

Santa Got Stuck in the Chimney

Poor Santa got stuck in our chimney.
I know it sounds weird, but it's true.
His feet made it down, but his belly
was one size too large for the flue.

His reindeer are up on our rooftop.
His sleigh is still loaded with toys.
And Santa, that kindly old fellow,
is making a whole lot of noise.

We called the police and the sheriff.
They showed up with ladders and cranes.
They brought all their winches and pulleys,
plus bungee cords, cables, and chains.

They're working right now to extract him
by hoisting him slowly back out.
It might take all day because Santa
is more than a little bit stout.

If you don't have presents this morning,
we're sorry you're having to wait.
But Santa's still stuck in our chimney.
He may be a day or two late.

Until then, please hide all your cookies,
though Santa may find this severe.
At least then he'll fit down the chimney
when he comes on Christmas next year.

Our Christmas Tree's Embarrassed

Our Christmas tree's embarrassed
and no doubt a little hurt,
for we've put him in the window,
and we've dressed him in a skirt.

We draped his boughs with pearls,
and I'm sure he thought, "Oh no!"
when atop his head we neatly tied
a big red velvet bow.

Our tree will feel much better when
we take these things from 'round him
and we plant him back out in the snow
as naked as we found him.

22

Christmas Sale

Here I am on Christmas day—
I'm glad at last it came,
but Christmas gifts from Mom and Dad
are often pretty lame.

It's all because my parents
won't buy gifts till they're on sale,
so this year I got Easter candy,
even though it's stale.

They saved a lot by buying stuff
the stores might throw away,
like all these shamrock-covered hats
from last St. Patrick's Day.

They also gave me valentines,
a Halloween mask, too,
and from the end-of-summer sale,
a charcoal barbecue.

I got a beach umbrella
to protect me from the sun.
It's ten degrees below outside;
just how can that be fun?

So, Mom and Dad, please understand
I'm saving money, too.
Next Christmas don't be too surprised
when these come back to you.

Christmas Dinner

Fruitcake.
Candied yams.
Mincemeat.
Roasted hams.
Eggnog.
Turkey legs.
Aspic.
Deviled eggs.
Gravy.
Dinner rolls.
Take some.
Pass the bowls.
Jell-O.
Christmas punch.
Cookies.
Munch, munch, munch.

Stuffing.
Gingerbread.
Whoops, I'm
overfed!
After
such a load,
feel like
I'll explode.
Guess I'm
gonna die,
so please
pass the pie.

Potluck Christmas

Aunt Agatha comes with a casserole dish
of dried-out spaghetti and overcooked fish,
and every Christmas I pray and I wish
Aunt Agatha won't bring her casserole dish.

My uncle Ernesto brings barbecued beans
that taste like a mush made of old magazines
combined with a crust from old rusted machines.
I wish that my uncle would not bring his beans.

My grandma brings aspic (that's Jell-O with shrimp),
and when I won't eat it she calls me a wimp.
I hope when they're dishing my dinner they skimp
on Grandma's inedible aspic with shrimp.

My mom makes a salad of peppers and peas
that's mixed up with onions and Limburger cheese.
As nice as I can, I say, "No, thank you, please."
Next Christmas why can't we just order Chinese?

The Day after Christmas

Wrapping paper everywhere,
and ribbons, tags, and bows
piled in our living room
as deep as winter snows.

Empty boxes, packages,
and bits of twine and tape
littered all across the floor.
It seems there's no escape.

Mistletoe, confetti,
and some scattered potpourri.
Tinsel, popcorn, ornaments,
and, yes, of course, the tree.

Now we're in a panic,
searching frantically all day.
We think we kept the garbage
and we threw the gifts away!

December 26

A BB gun.
A model plane.
A basketball.
A 'lectric train.

A bicycle.
A cowboy hat.
A comic book.
A baseball bat.

A deck of cards.
A science kit.
A racing car.
A catcher's mitt.

So that's my list
of everything
that Santa Claus
forgot to bring.

Resolutions

My New Year's resolutions are
to lounge upon the couch.
To spit out things like okra and
permit myself to slouch.
To make the famous Guinness book
for days without a bath.
To get the A's in recess that
I'll never get in math.
To seldom raise my hand in class
and try my very best
to fake convincing illnesses
the night before a test.

To trade my lunch away when
I have liverwurst on rye.
To clean my bedroom thoroughly
on days that start with *Y*.
To gather fuzzy lint between
my toes for several weeks.
To run from Aunt Petunia when
she tries to pinch my cheeks.
To stay in my pajamas for
as long as I can stand.
To learn to burp the alphabet
the way I've always planned.
Experience has taught me well
that I will have success
with all my resolutions
if I simply strive for less.

Library of Congress Cataloging-in-Publication Data

Nesbitt, Kenn.
  Santa got stuck in the chimney : 20 funny poems full of Christmas cheer / by Kenn Nesbitt and Linda Knaus ; illustrated by Mike and Carl Gordon.
      p. cm.
  Summary: "A collection of 20 humorous poems about Christmas"—Provided by publisher.
  ISBN 0-88166-515-0 (Meadowbrook Press) ISBN 1-41692-201-6 (Simon & Schuster)
  1. Christmas—Juvenile poetry. 2. Children's poetry, American. I. Knaus, Linda, 1961- II. Gordon, Mike, ill. III. Gordon, Carl, ill. IV. Title.
  PS3614.E47S36 2006
  811'.6080334—dc22

                    2006000674

Project Director: Bruce Lansky
Editorial Director: Christine Zuchora-Walske
Coordinating Editor and Copyeditor: Angela Wiechmann
Proofreaders: Alicia Ester, Megan McGinnis
Production Manager: Paul Woods
Graphic Design Manager: Tamara Peterson
Illustrations and Cover Art: Mike and Carl Gordon

Poem Credits
pp. 12, 27 © 2001 by Kenn Nesbitt; p. 24 © 2004 by Kenn Nesbitt; pp. 2, 6 © 2005 by Kenn Nesbitt; pp. 1, 10, 16, 20, 25 © 2006 by Kenn Nesbitt; p. 4 © 2004 by Linda Knaus; pp. 8, 14, 15, 19, 22, 28 © 2006 by Linda Knaus; pp. 9, 23, 26 © 2006 by Kenn Nesbitt and Linda Knaus.

Published by Meadowbrook Press, 5451 Smetana Drive, Minnetonka, Minnesota 55343

www.meadowbrookpress.com

BOOK TRADE DISTRIBUTION by Simon and Schuster, a division of Simon and Schuster, Inc., 1230 Avenue of the Americas, New York, New York 10020

12 11 10 09 08 07 06   10 9 8 7 6 5 4 3 2 1

Printed in Malaysia

Acknowledgments
Many thanks to the following teachers and their students who tested poems for this collection: Meredith Andrews, Diane Czajak, Kathy Kenney-Marshall, Andrea Rutkowski, and Patricia Towle of McCarthy Elementary, Framingham, MA.